Ticks

and what you can do about them

Roger Drummond, Ph.D.

WILDERNESS PRESS · BERKELEY, CA

Ticks and What You Can Do About them

1st EDITION May 1990
2nd EDITION April 1998
3rd EDITION March 2004

Copyright © 1990, 1998, 2004 by Roger Drummond, Ph.D.

Book design: Andreas Schueller
Book editors: Jessica Benner, Elaine Merrill

ISBN 0-89997- 353-1
UPC 7-19609-97353-9

Manufactured in the United States of America

Published by: **Wilderness Press**
1200 5th Street
Berkeley, CA 94710
(800) 443-7227; FAX (510) 558-1696
info@wildernesspress.com
www.wildernesspress.com

Visit our website for a complete listing of our books and for ordering information.

SAFETY NOTICE: Although Wilderness Press and the author have made every attempt to ensure that the information in this book is accurate at press time, they are not responsible for any loss, damage, injury, or inconvenience that may occur as a result of using this book. The information contained here is no substitute for professional advice or training. Readers are encouraged to seek medical help whenever possible.

Contents

Acknowledgments, Third Edition

The author wishes to thank persons who provided information, help, and advice for any or all of the three editions of this book. Dr. Glen Needham, Institute of Acarology, The Ohio State University, Columbus, Ohio, provided the picture of the mouthparts, Maps 1 and 2, and also reviewed a draft. Dr. James Keirans, Institute of Arthropodology and Parasitology, Georgia Southern University, Statesboro, Ga., reviewed the maps. Dr. Mat Pound and Ms. Chris Santos, Knipling-Bushland U.S. Livestock Insects Research Laboratory, Kerrville, Tex., updated the maps for the second and third editions and reviewed a draft. Dr. Joseph Piesman, Division of Vector-borne Infectious Diseases, CDC Fort Collins, Colo., provided Map 3 and reviewed a draft. EcoHealth, Inc., Boston, Mass., provided the plate of the actual size of the blacklegged tick. Dr. Willy Burgdorfer, Dike Drummond, M.D., Don Drummond, Dr. Lance Durden, Dr. John George, Maud Jennings, Dr. Sam Junkin, Dr. Robert Lane, Dr. Robert Miller, Dr. Dan Sonenshine, Richard Stewart, David Weld, and Rita Wilson read final drafts. Special thanks to Joe Fleming for his insightful review of this third edition. Roslyn Bullas, Managing Editor, Elaine Merrill, Editor, Jessica Benner, Editorial Assistant, and Andreas Schueller, Designer, all of Wilderness Press, provided constructive editorial advice. My most helpful advice, comments, and criticism came from Ellen Drummond, friend, companion, and wife.

Introduction

Have you or members of your family found a tick crawling on or attached to you or them? Do you want to know how to remove an attached tick? Have you become aware of the diseases, especially Lyme disease and Rocky Mountain spotted fever, carried by ticks? Do you live in an area or are you planning to visit an area that has ticks? Have you read an article about ticks and the diseases they carry and want to know more? Are you looking for ways to keep ticks from getting on you and your family? Are you or your community looking for ways to control ticks and have you heard or read about new methods and materials used to control ticks on mice and deer? This book gives detailed information on how you can protect yourself from ticks, how you can remove attached ticks safely, and how you can control ticks.

This book tells about ticks—what they are, how and where they live, the diseases they carry, and the problems they cause.

Nature and all outdoors are to be enjoyed. As with any part of life, this enjoyment is not without its risks. One of these risks is the presence of ticks and tick-carried diseases. A tick bite can cause severe irritation and even paralysis. If you know more about ticks and how you can protect yourself and your family from them, you and they can enjoy the outdoors with a greatly reduced risk of contacting ticks and suffering from tick-carried diseases. The first six chapters of this book give information on ticks and the diseases they carry. The last three chapters provide practical measures you can take to reduce the risks from ticks and tick-carried diseases.

Chapter 1.
Ticks and How They Live

Ticks are part of a large group of animals that have jointed legs and skeletons located on the outside of their bodies. This group, called arthropods, includes insects, crustaceans, myriapods, and arachnids. Arachnids, in turn, include spiders, scorpions, mites, and ticks. Scientists have described more than 850 kinds of ticks in the world and 100 of these carry organisms that cause diseases of wildlife, livestock, pets, and people.

Ticks' only food is the blood they suck from their hosts (usually warm-blooded animals).

The front part of a tick consists of the "head" area which contains the mouthparts. The mouthparts have a central structure, the hypostome, which is shaped like a harpoon, flat on the top and curved on the bottom, with many recurved barbs, and two chelicerae which have sharp teeth on their front ends. Plate 1 is a scanning electron photomicrograph of a tick's mouthparts. A tick cuts an opening in the skin of a host with the teeth on the end of its chelicerae and then pushes its hypostome into the hole it has made. At the same time, the tick secretes a cement-like substance in and around the opening. The barbs on the hypostome and the cement anchor the tick to the host's skin and make it difficult to remove once it has attached. The teeth on the chelicerae then cut blood vessels under the skin, causing the blood to form a pool. To keep the blood from clotting, ticks inject saliva containing an anticoagulant into the pool of blood. The tick then sucks this blood into its gut through the hypostome. The saliva may also contain disease organisms, so removing a tick as soon as you discover it is important to avoiding getting a tick-carried disease.

The rear part of a tick consists of the body, which is designed to expand as the tick takes in blood. When a tick feeds, the tick's gut enlarges as it receives blood, and the accordion-like skin of the tick's body grows and unfolds as the gut increases in size. Some female ticks can increase their size 20-50 times and their weight more than 200 times as they feed. Male ticks increase only slightly.

Ticks go through four stages in their life cycle—adult, egg, larva, and nymph. The adult stage consists of sexually mature, eight-legged male and female ticks. The adult sexes usually differ in color, size, and appearance: females are usually larger and more colorful than males. Females and males emit chemicals, called sex pheromones, to attract the opposite sex. These pheromones allow adults to find each other and act as an aid to mating. Adults find hosts, attach, suck blood, and mate. Some adults attach and suck blood only once; others do so several times. Mating may take place on or off a host and before or after feeding.

Fully fed, mated females lay eggs. Females die after laying all their eggs.

Some females feed once and lay all their eggs in a single mass containing thousands of eggs, while others feed several times and lay eggs in several small batches after each feeding.

Males usually feed slightly and live to mate several females.

Eggs hatch into very tiny six-legged larvae, often called seed ticks. A larva finds a host, attaches, and sucks blood until full. When full, it detaches and drops to the ground. After a week or so, the larva changes form, in a process called molting, and becomes a nymph. A nymph is larger than a larva, has eight legs, but still does not have sex organs. The nymph breaks out of the larval skin, finds a host, attaches, and sucks blood. Some nymphs feed several times and molt to another nymph before finally feeding, dropping off the host, and then molting to an adult. Other nymphs feed only once, drop off, and molt to an adult. The adult breaks out of the nymphal skin and finds a host.

Ticks have a unique system for finding hosts. They have sense organs on their front legs that detect carbon dioxide, host odors, and heat given off by warm-blooded animals. Using these sense organs, ticks locate and can crawl to hosts. Researchers and health officials use this behavior to collect ticks. They place a small block of dry ice on a cloth, the dry ice sublimates to carbon dioxide, the ticks detect the carbon dioxide and crawl to the cloth. Some ticks may crawl 10-15 or more feet to a source of carbon dioxide. Ticks do not fly to or jump onto their hosts; they are only found on or near the ground.

Ticks are divided into two families—soft ticks and hard ticks. Soft ticks do not have a hard shield on any part of their body. The entire body of a soft tick can expand during feeding. Because of their shape and their wrinkled skin, when they have fed on blood, soft ticks look like little raisins. Soft ticks usually

There are over 150 kinds of soft ticks.

live in sheltered places, such as burrows and nests of their hosts. Larvae feed only once, but feeding may last a week or more. Nymphs and adults usually feed several times, but each feeding may last less than an hour. Mating takes place off the host after the adults have fed. Female soft ticks lay small batches of 50-200 eggs after each feeding and then die.

Hard ticks have a hard shield that covers all or part of their bodies. In the female, this shield covers only about the front third of her back, and the rest of her body can expand greatly as she feeds. In the male, this shield covers most of his back, and his body can expand only slightly as he feeds. Hard ticks are usually found outdoors. Each stage feeds only once, for three days to several weeks. Mating usually takes place on the host before or during feeding. Fully fed females lay eggs in the environment in a single mass, which can be as large as 20,000 eggs, and then they die. There are over 650 kinds of hard ticks.

Ticks are important because they can be a nuisance and also carry organisms that may cause diseases in wildlife, livestock, pets, and people. Although colonists in the eastern U.S. found many ticks, there is no record that these settlers were affected by any tick-carried diseases. A traveler in New York state in 1749 wrote that it was impossible to sit without being attacked by an army of ticks. Clearing of the eastern forests, which changed the environment, and hunting of large and small wild animals, which lowered the number of tick hosts, caused a decrease in the number of ticks. A visitor to the same area in 1872 noted that the common tick had become nearly extinct.

There were, however, tick-human diseases in the early West. Native Americans living in the Rocky

Mountains recognized places with "evil spirits" (apparently ticks) that should be avoided or first traveled by squaws to remove the problem (pick up the ticks). Prospectors, hunters, and settlers entered and lived in these areas and were fed upon by ticks that carried disease-causing organisms. Although Rocky Mountain spotted fever is still found in the Rocky Mountains, today almost all cases are reported in southeastern and south-central states rather than western states.

The first recognized tick-carried human disease in the U.S. was Rocky Mountain spotted fever.

In 1975, a new human disease carried by ticks was found in the U.S. This disease, called Lyme disease, is now a major health problem in some areas of the northeast, the upper Midwest, and the Pacific Coast. Several other tick-carried human diseases are also found in the U.S. The rickettsias, viruses, bacteria, and protozoa that cause these diseases develop inside ticks and are injected into persons while ticks feed.

Some ticks do not carry a disease but are a nuisance and can cause itching, swelling, redness, and sometimes pain when they "bite" a person. Actually, ticks don't bite; they attach to a host by sticking their mouthparts into the host's skin. When you scrape an attached tick off, sometimes you break off these mouthparts, which remain in the skin and can cause irritation and secondary infection.

Feeding by certain ticks can cause paralysis. This condition, called tick paralysis, is the result of a toxin injected into a person as the tick feeds. Paralysis spreads from the legs and arms and can lead to death. Once the feeding tick is found and removed, the paralysis abates, and the person usually recovers rapidly.

Chapter 2.
Where Ticks Live

Ticks live wherever their hosts live. Like all parasites, ticks cannot live without hosts. A few ticks feed on only one kind of host, while most ticks can suck blood from many different animals. When not attached to and feeding on their hosts, most hard ticks live outdoors on the ground in grass, woods, brush, weeds, etc. They are found in the leaf litter and duff on the soil. One unique hard tick, the brown dog tick, can live inside houses, kennels, or wherever dogs live. Soft ticks usually live in the nests, burrows, houses, or caves where their hosts live.

Ticks are not uniformly distributed throughout the environment. Usually the largest numbers and variety of ticks are found where the largest numbers and variety of wild animal hosts are found. Most hosts live around water, on the edges of open areas in forests and wooded areas in prairies. Humans change the environment when they cut down trees in the forest or plant trees on the prairie. These changes can lead to more "edge" areas for wildlife and thus to a larger number of ticks. People also put domesticated animals, especially cattle, on limited, fenced pasture areas. Some ticks that usually feed on wildlife may also feed on livestock. If so, their number may increase to many times the number supported by wildlife alone. In contrast, when people destroy the forest, plow the prairie, overgraze the land, and decrease numbers of wild animals, the number of ticks in that area may decrease because of the lack of hosts or of suitable places for ticks to live, molt, and lay eggs.

There are a number of examples of changes in the dynamics of a tick-carried disease because of human activities in the environment. One example is Rocky Mountain spotted fever. Rocky Mountain spotted fever became a problem with the settling of the West in the late 1800s. Over time, humans cleared much of the land and changed it to pastures and fields. As a result, the number and the distribution of the Rocky Mountain wood tick, a carrier of the disease, decreased, which caused a decrease in the number of cases of the disease in the Rocky Mountains. Now Rocky Mountain spotted fever in the West is usually acquired in forested and rural areas where lumbermen, sportsmen, hikers, campers, and others contact disease-carrying ticks.

In the 1940s, more cases of Rocky Mountain spotted fever were found in the southeast than in the West. Since 1964, more than 90% of all recorded cases of this disease have occurred east of the Rockies. In the last 50 years people have been moving from southeastern cities to suburbs and rural areas, where they encountered disease-carrying ticks. Also, in the southeast, with the abandoning of large farms and the regrowth of limited woods, there are more wildlife hosts and more places for ticks to live than in the past.

The tick that carries Rocky Mountain spotted fever in the southeast is the American dog tick. The wooded yards and small farms of the suburbanites created new areas for wildlife, good hosts for the American dog tick. Suburbanites also brought their pets, especially dogs, which are excellent hosts for this tick, and can bring disease-carrying ticks into homes, so a person need not go outdoors to get Rocky Mountain spotted fever. Chapter 5 has more information on Rocky Mountain spotted fever.

Another example of ticks' response to human activity is the relatively recent appearance of Lyme disease in the U.S. Although known in Europe since the late 1800s, physicians first diagnosed this disease in the U.S. in 1975 in Old Lyme, Connecticut, as Lyme arthritis. The organism that causes Lyme disease is present in the blood of wild animals, especially mice. Two kinds of ticks, the blacklegged tick, found in the northeast, southeast, and upper Midwest, and the western blacklegged tick, found in the Pacific Coast states, pick up this disease when they feed on mice and carry it to persons. Other ticks carry Lyme disease among wildlife but do not attack persons.

It is speculated that the blacklegged tick was present throughout the northern part of its range from Minnesota to the Atlantic Ocean when this area was covered with trees and had many white-tailed deer. During the 1800s, clearing the land reduced tick habitat and unregulated hunting reduced the number of deer, leading to a large decrease in the number and distribution of the blacklegged tick. Over the past 40 years, however, an increase in wooded areas, the regulation of hunting, and wildlife-conservation efforts have caused an increase in tick habitat and in populations of deer and other wildlife. As a result, the number and the distribution of the blacklegged tick have increased. At the same time, people moved to the suburbs and to rural areas and found deer, mice, and blacklegged ticks. Blacklegged ticks feed on mice and become infected with the organism that causes Lyme disease. Infected ticks then feed on people and wildlife. Because of increases in the numbers of wild animals and infected blacklegged ticks, more people are exposed to ticks and Lyme disease. In recent years, due to greater public and medical awareness of this disease, there has been a continuing increase in the number of reported cases of Lyme disease. Chapter 4 has further information on Lyme disease.

In the late 1980s and early 1990s, two other closely related tick-carried diseases were found in the U.S. Unfortunately, they don't have simple common names like Lyme disease and Rocky Mountain spotted fever. One is human monocytic ehrlichiosis (HME), found mainly in south-central and southeastern states, and carried by the lone star tick. The other is human granulocytic ehrlichiosis (HGE), found in the upper Midwestern and New England states, and carried by the blacklegged tick. Both these diseases are also reported in California. Chapter 6 has detailed information on these two diseases, on another new, recently discovered kind of ehrlichiosis, and other tick-carried diseases.

Chapter 3.
Important Ticks

There are 83 kinds of ticks in the U.S. Of these, seven kinds of hard ticks and five kinds of soft ticks carry diseases, are a nuisance, or cause paralysis. Table 1 lists ticks found in all states except Alaska and Hawaii. Alaska has the Rocky Mountain wood tick outdoors and the brown dog tick indoors. Hawaii has the brown dog tick. The District of Columbia will have the ticks found in Maryland and Virginia.

A. Lone star tick
Amblyomma americanum

The unfed female of this hard tick has a white mark, the "lone star," on the shield in the front of her back (Plate 2). The rest of her body is reddish-brown. The smaller, unfed male is the same color, with pale lacy white markings on the rear edge of the shield that covers all of his back (PLATE 2). The much smaller larvae and nymphs are reddish-brown.

Adults are active in spring and early summer. Larvae are active in late summer. Nymphs are active from spring until fall. Adults and nymphs survive winter buried in the soil. Larvae and nymphs feed on many small animals; adults and nymphs feed on many large animals. All stages feed on deer and people.

🕷

Table 1. Important ticks found in 48 states

State	Hard Ticks							Soft Ticks	
	Lone Star	Rocky Mt.	Pacific Coast	Amer. Dog	Blacklegged	Western BL	Brown Dog	Relap. Fever	Pajahuello
AL	●			●	●		●		
AZ		●				●	●	●	
AR	●			●	●		●		
CA		●	●	●		●	●	●	●
CO		●					●	●	
CT	●			●	●		●		
DE	●			●	●		●		
FL	●			●	●		●	●	
GA	●			●	●		●		
ID		●		●			●	●	
IL	●			●	●		●		
IN	●			●	●		●		
IA	●			●	●		●		
KS	●			●	●		●	●	
KY	●			●	●		●		
LA	●			●	●		●		
MA	●			●	●		●		
MD	●			●	●		●		
ME	●			●	●		●		
MI				●	●		●		
MN				●	●		●		
MS	●			●	●		●		
MO	●			●	●		●		
MT		●		●			●	●	
NE		●		●	●		●		
NV		●	●			●	●	●	●
NH	●			●	●		●		
NJ	●			●	●		●		
NM		●				●	●		

Table 1. *(continued)*

| | Hard Ticks | | | | | | | Soft Ticks | |
State	Lone Star	Rocky Mt.	Pacific Coast	Amer. Dog	Blacklegged	Western BL	Brown Dog	Relap. Fever	Pajahuello
NY	●			●	●		●		
NC	●			●	●		●		
ND		●		●	●		●		
OH	●			●	●		●		
OK	●			●	●		●	●	
OR		●	●	●		●	●	●	
PA	●			●	●		●		
RI	●			●	●		●		
SC	●			●	●		●		
SD		●		●	●		●		
TN	●			●	●		●		
TX	●			●	●		●	●	
UT		●				●	●	●	
VT	●			●	●		●		
VA	●			●	●		●		
WA		●				●	●	●	
WV	●			●	●		●		
WI				●	●		●		
WY		●					●		●

The lone star tick is found throughout the southeastern third of the U.S. and into New England (Map 1). In eastern Oklahoma, it is estimated that this tick kills 20-40% of white-tailed deer fawns born each year. Ticks attach around the eyes and their feeding causes the skin there to swell and bleed. Fawns with many ticks on them go blind, die, or become so weak they are killed by predators.

Map 1

Probable distributions of:

the lone star tick

the Pacific Coast tick

People who walk through vegetation that contains a clump of lone star larvae, called seed ticks, may find many tiny ticks crawling on them. All stages of ticks usually attach to the skin under tight places, such as underwear, bra straps, and belts. Ticks crawl on the skin and attach when they are stopped by tight clothing. People usually scrape off larvae during bathing or showering if done soon after contact with the ticks. If not removed, attached ticks can cause a rash and itching and the attachment site may become inflamed and infected. Lone star ticks have long mouthparts and are difficult to remove once firmly attached.

The lone star tick is a very aggressive tick.

Lone star ticks are the principal carriers of human monocytic ehrlichiosis (HME) and one of the carriers of tularemia. Because they are aggressive feeders and are often found on people, lone star ticks have been suspected as carriers of other diseases. True, organisms that cause Rocky Mountain spotted fever have been found in lone star ticks, but there is no proof this tick gives this disease to people. Recently, a Lyme disease-like illness, named Southern Tick-Associated Rash Illness (STARI) has been associated with attached lone star ticks. Also, another recently recognized ehrlichiosis, caused by *Ehrlichia ewingii*, found only in a few cases in Missouri, Oklahoma, and Tennessee, is carried by lone star ticks.

B. Rocky Mountain wood tick
Dermacentor andersoni

This hard tick looks like the Pacific Coast tick and the American dog tick (Plate 3). The unfed female has silvery gray markings on the shield on the front third of her back; the rest is reddish-brown. The unfed male has silvery gray markings on the shield on all of his back. Larvae and nymphs are dark reddish-brown.

Adults usually overwinter buried in the soil and become active in early summer. Larvae also are active in summer. Nymphs may be active in summer or they may overwinter in the soil and become active in spring. Larvae and nymphs feed on a variety of small animals. Adults feed on many large animals.

The Rocky Mountain wood tick is found in the Rocky Mountain states, west to the eastern slope of the Cascade Mountains, and south to New Mexico and Arizona (Map 2). In the Pacific states, it is usually found only in the higher elevations. It is the prime carrier of Rocky Mountain spotted fever in the West and also carries tularemia and Colorado tick fever. It is the most frequent cause of tick paralysis in the U.S.

C. Pacific Coast tick
Dermacentor occidentalis

This hard tick looks like the Rocky Mountain wood tick and the American dog tick (Plate 3). The unfed female has a silvery gray pattern on the shield on her back; the rest of her body is reddish-brown. The unfed male has silvery gray markings on the shield on all his back. Larvae and nymphs are dark brown.

Adults are active from fall through late spring. Larvae and nymphs are active in late spring and summer. Larvae and nymphs feed on a variety of small animals, while adults feed on large animals.

The Pacific Coast tick is found in California, southeastern Oregon, and northwestern Nevada, west of the

Map 2

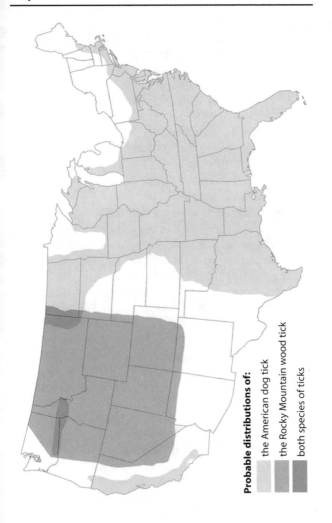

Probable distributions of:

the American dog tick

the Rocky Mountain wood tick

both species of ticks

Continental Divide (Map 1). It carries tularemia and Rocky Mountain spotted fever and is a suspected carrier of Colorado tick fever.

D. American dog tick
Dermacentor variabilis

In many places this tick is called the wood tick. The unfed female (Plate 3) has silvery gray markings on the shield on the front third of her back; the rest of her body is reddish-brown. Female American dog ticks look like the female Rocky Mountain wood tick and Pacific Coast tick. The unfed male (Plate 3) has silvery gray markings on the shield covering all of his back. Larvae are a dull yellow and nymphs are reddish-brown.

Adults overwinter in the soil and are active from spring to fall. Larvae are active in spring and summer. Nymphs are active in summer and may overwinter. Larvae and nymphs feed on mice and many other small animals. Adults feed on many medium-sized and large animals, including dogs and people.

The American dog tick is widely distributed in the eastern half of the U.S. and is also found on the West Coast (Map 2). It is the most common carrier of Rocky Mountain spotted fever in the southeast. It also carries tularemia, may be a carrier of human granulocytic ehrlichiosis, and also causes tick paralysis in persons and dogs.

E. Blacklegged tick
Ixodes scapularis

In the northeast, this tick was described in 1979 as the deer tick, *Ixodes dammini*. Since then, scientists have shown the deer tick is actually the blacklegged tick. In the northeast, this tick is still often called the deer tick because it was first found on deer, while in the Midwest, it is often called the bear tick because it was first found on bears. The unfed female (Plate 4) is very dark reddish-brown and has no markings on her back, although the shield on the front third of her body is visible. The unfed male (Plate 4) is black. Males and females have black legs; other ticks generally have brown legs. Larvae are very dark colored and nymphs are dark reddish-brown. The blacklegged tick is very small. Larvae are about the size of the period at the end of this sentence. Nymphs are about the size of a poppy seed, and adults are about one-eighth inch long. Actual sizes of all stages of the blacklegged tick are shown in Figure 1.

Figure 1. Blacklegged Ticks (*Ixodes scapularis*)

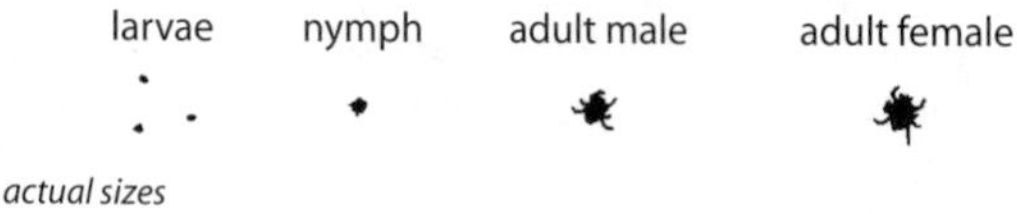

larvae	nymph	adult male	adult female

actual sizes

Adults may feed in the fall or in warm weather in early winter and late spring.

Adults and larvae may overwinter in the soil and find hosts in spring. Nymphs are active all summer. Larvae and nymphs feed on mice and other mammals, ground-frequenting birds, skinks, and lizards. Adults feed on deer, cattle, dogs, and other medium-to-large animals. All stages, especially nymphs and adults, have been found attached to people.

The blacklegged tick is found widely distributed in the eastern two thirds of the U.S. into Canada, west to the Dakotas and south into Mexico (Map 3). Each year it is discovered in more locations. In the U.S., this tick is the most frequent carrier of Lyme disease, human granulocytic ehrlichiosis, and human babesiosis.

F. Western blacklegged tick
Ixodes pacificus

Unfed females and males look like blacklegged ticks (Plate 4). Females are dark reddish-brown and males are black. Both have black legs. Larvae and nymphs are dark reddish-brown. This tick is the same size as the blacklegged tick (Figure 1).

Adults are active from November through May. Larvae and nymphs are active in late winter to summer. Larvae and nymphs feed on lizards, birds, and other small animals; adults feed on medium to large animals including man.

This tick is found along the Pacific Coast as well as in parts of Nevada, Utah, and Arizona (Map 3). It is the carrier of Lyme disease and human granulocytic ehrlichiosis in the far western U.S.

G. Brown dog tick
Rhipicephalus sanguineus

The unfed female of this hard tick is brown (Plate 5). The shield on the front third of her back is darker than the rest of her body. The unfed male is a uniform dark brown (Plate 5). As females feed, their color changes to a brownish gray. Unfed larvae and nymphs are dark brown.

The brown dog tick is found throughout the U.S. wherever you find dogs. All stages of this tick can be found indoors. Fed females lay eggs in secluded places,

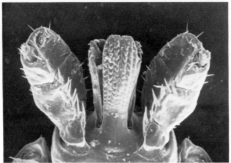

Plate 1. A scanning electron microphotograph of the mouthparts of the American dog tick. The central structure is the hypostome.

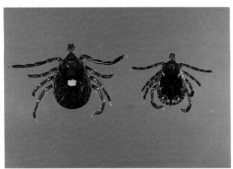

Plate 2. Color photograph of adults of the lone star tick. Female left and male right. Actual size about 1/4 inch long.

Plate 3. Color photograph of adults of the American dog tick. Female left and male right. Actual size about 1/4 inch long.

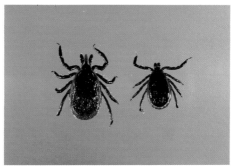

Plate 4. Color photograph of adults of the black-legged tick. Female left and male right. Actual size about 1/8 inch long.

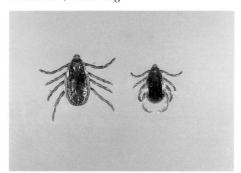

Plate 5. Color photograph of adults of the brown dog tick. Female left and male right. Actual size about 3/16th inch long.

Plate 6. Color photograph of an adult relapsing fever tick. Actual size about 1/4 inch long.

Map 3

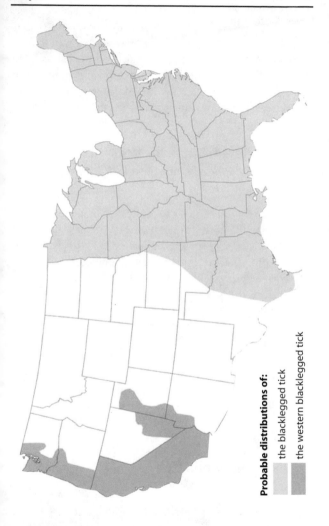

Probable distributions of:

the blacklegged tick

the western blacklegged tick

and fed larvae and nymphs drop off dogs and molt in any sheltered place. Unfed larvae, nymphs, and adults crawl on and may try to attach to people, though attachment is uncommon. Populations of brown dog ticks can increase to enormous numbers in places where dogs are kept and this tick can be a major household pest.

H. Relapsing fever ticks

Ornithodoros hermsi, O. parkeri, O. talaje, and O. turicata

These four kinds of soft ticks look alike and have similar life cycles. Adults are gray to pale blue, and their oval-shaped soft bodies have a rough texture (Plate 6). Larvae and nymphs are gray.

Relapsing fever ticks are found widely scattered west of the Mississippi River in nests and burrows of many small animals, especially rodents. *O. turicata* lives in Florida in burrows of wild and feral pigs and in nests of gopher tortoises.

Relapsing fever ticks can live without feeding for 5-10 years. People entering their habitats are regularly attacked by hungry ticks if normal hosts are not available. The bite of these ticks can be painful.

As the name implies these ticks carry tick-borne relapsing fever.

I. Pajahuello tick

Ornithodoros coriaceus

This soft tick looks like a relapsing fever tick (Plate 6). It is found in bedding grounds of deer and cattle.

All stages feed on deer, cattle and other hosts; nymphs and adults attach to people.

The pajahuello tick is found in California and Nevada and was originally called *pajaronela* by natives of the Santa Lucia mountain range in coastal California. This tick carries no human diseases (it carries an important disease of cattle) but its bite can cause severe reactions in many people. Usually a localized reaction of pain and swelling occurs where the tick has attached and fed. These symptoms usually disappear in two days, but often a small knot remains at the site, which usually disappears in one to two weeks. Persons allergic to the bite may have severe reactions with swelling, pain, and redness that may require medical attention and take up to several months to disappear.

Chapter 4.
Lyme Disease

Physicians first diagnosed Lyme disease in the U.S. in 1975 in Old Lyme, Connecticut, where they found an unusual arthritis in children. This disease has been known since the 1880s in Europe, where it is called *erythema migrans*, which means migrating red rash. Lyme disease had been present, but not diagnosed, in Wisconsin in 1970. It was found in California in 1978. It is caused by the spirochete, *Borrelia burgdorferi*. In the U.S., the number of reported cases of Lyme disease has increased almost every year since 1982, when the Center for Disease Control and Prevention (CDC) of the U.S. Department of Health and Human Services declared it a reportable disease. Lyme disease, now the most commonly reported tick-carried disease in the U.S., is concentrated in certain parts of the country. States with the highest rates of occurrence are Connecticut, Rhode Island, New York, New Jersey, Delaware, and Pennsylvania. Table 2 shows the reported cases of Lyme disease from 1982-2002. Even though over 200,000 cases have been reported, it is speculated that in areas where it is common, Lyme disease may be underreported, and in areas where it is uncommon, it may be overreported. It is also known that underdiagnosis and misdiagnosis of Lyme disease occur, therefore it is possible that cases have occurred that were not diagnosed and not reported.

Table 2. Reported cases of Lyme disease*

State	1982-1999	2000	2001	2002	Total
New York	50121	4329	4083	5535	64068
Connecticut	23375	3773	3597	4631	35376
New Jersey	16673	2492	2020	2349	23534
Pennsylvania	18134	2343	2804	3989	27267
Wisconsin	6143	631	597	1090	8461
Rest of the states	30703	4162	3926	6170	44961
All states	145149	17730	17027	23764	203670

*1982-2002, from five states with the highest numbers, rest of the states, and all the states. Data furnished by CDC (provisional for 2002).

Distribution

Lyme disease is concentrated in three areas of the U.S.: the northeast, from Maryland to Maine, where most cases occur, the upper Midwest, especially Wisconsin and Minnesota, and on the Pacific Coast in California and Oregon. Over 92% of all reported cases occurred in 10 states—California, Connecticut, Maryland, Massachusetts, Minnesota, New Jersey, New York, Pennsylvania, Rhode Island, and Wisconsin. However, cases of Lyme disease have been reported in all the other states, as well as Guam and Puerto Rico.

Symptoms

The symptoms of Lyme disease usually appear in three stages. The first-stage, or acute, symptoms usually appear between three days and three weeks after an infected tick has attached to a person. Symptoms usually consist of an expanding ring-like, bull's-eye red rash, called *erythema migrans*, on the skin, usually where the feeding tick attached. This rash appears in 60 to 80% of infected persons. Often the rash is red around the edges with a clear center. Secondary rashes may be found some distance away from the original rash. The person also has flu-like symptoms such as fever, fatigue, chills, headaches, a stiff neck, and muscle aches and pains. These symptoms often disappear after several weeks.

Lyme disease is called the great imitator because its symptoms imitate the symptoms of many other diseases.

The second- and third-stage, or chronic, symptoms may occur separately or together, weeks or months after the first stage symptoms. Second-stage symptoms may include skin lesions, meningitis, severe headaches, stiff neck, encephalitis, paralysis of facial muscles, abnormal heart beat, numbness, withdrawal, loss of confidence, lethargy, and other symptoms. These symptoms may last for several weeks or months and then disappear.

Third-stage symptoms, which may occur months or years later, include arthritis in large joints, especially the knee, with swelling, pain, and stiffness. Arthritis may become chronic and in children is sometimes mistaken for juvenile rheumatoid arthritis. Other symptoms include fatigue, numbness, loss of memory, and irregular heart beat. These symptoms may also mimic symptoms of multiple sclerosis or Alzheimer's disease.

Early diagnosis of Lyme disease is contingent on finding an attached tick and the rash or, if there is no rash, the flu-like symptoms. Specific blood tests can determine if a person is infected. Treatment with specific antibiotics given during the first stage of the disease can almost always eliminate the disease and decrease severity of later symptoms. Antibiotics can also treat second- and third-stage symptoms. Persons in areas with Lyme disease must check themselves for ticks and a rash or flu-like symptoms in the summer. Prompt medical attention and treatment can prevent or lessen the long-term effects of Lyme disease. Lyme disease is rarely fatal, but the arthritis and other late stage symptoms can be very debilitating, severe, and long-lasting.

Vaccine for Lyme disease

In December of 1998, the Food and Drug Administration (FDA) approved an adjuvated recombinant vaccine (LYMErix®), and in January of 1999 GlaxoSmithKline Pharmaceuticals started marketing the product. Clinical trials showed that a three dose treatment at the first, second, and twelfth months provided some 76% protection against the disease. The vaccine was recommended for persons aged 15 to 70 who live, work, or recreate in areas of moderate to high risk of Lyme disease and who are exposed to tick-infested habitat. Unfortunately, a number of persons who had been vaccinated reported side effects similar to the arthritis caused by Lyme disease. Citing lack of sales, GlaxoSmithKline withdrew the vaccine from the market in February of 2002. A class-action lawsuit was settled in July of 2003.

Tick carriers and the disease cycle

The blacklegged tick, in the northeast and the Midwest, and the western blacklegged tick, along the Pacific Coast, are the only proven carriers of human Lyme disease. These small ticks (Figure 1) are hard to see. Larvae and nymphs take in spirochetes as they feed on infected mice. Infected larvae engorge with blood, drop off the host and molt to infected nymphs, and infected nymphs molt to infected adults. Infected nymphs and adults inject spirochetes into people as they feed, transmitting Lyme disease. More cases of Lyme disease in people are the result of the feeding of infected nymphs than of infected adults, probably because adults are easier to see and remove than nymphs. Most cases of Lyme disease occur between late spring and midsummer, when people are outdoors and nymphs are most active.

In laboratory tests, the lone star tick and the American dog tick did not transmit Lyme disease after feeding on infected hosts, and are not considered carriers of the disease.

Lyme disease has been diagnosed in dogs, horses, and other domestic animals. A vaccine has been developed to protect dogs from the disease.

Cases of Lyme disease often appear in places that normally do not have the disease or the tick carriers. Recent research in Canada has shown that blacklegged ticks, even lone star ticks, are transported north while attached to and feeding on migrating birds. Infected ticks attach to birds in an area where the ticks and the disease are found and, after the birds migrate, the ticks finish feeding and drop off hosts in an area where neither the ticks nor the disease had previously been found. There the ticks molt and can give Lyme disease to persons when they feed on them. Ticks can even be transported on horses, cats, dogs, and other pets. Therefore, it is very important that persons and physicians in areas not known to have Lyme disease quickly recognize its symptoms so the disease can be detected and treated early. Even though a great deal is known, much remains to be learned about diagnosis, treatment, distribution, and carriers of Lyme disease.

Also of importance to note is the possibility of co-infection with Lyme disease, human babesiosis, and human granulocytic ehrlichiosis. Co-infection has been recorded in the upper Midwest and the northeastern states in both ticks and persons. If a person has two or even three of these diseases at the same time, symptoms may be confusing; specific diagnosis is complicated and may depend upon critical blood tests. To get the appropriate treatment, it is necessary to diagnose each disease correctly.

Chapter 5.
Rocky Mountain Spotted Fever

First recognized as a disease in the 1890s, Rocky Mountain spotted fever was the first diagnosed tick-carried human disease in the U.S. It was called Rocky Mountain spotted fever because it was found in the Rocky Mountains, and infected persons had a rash with red-purple-black spots. This disease, caused by a rickettsia, *Rickettsia rickettsii*, is carried by the Rocky Mountain wood tick and the American dog tick. The CDC reported the number of cases increased almost every year until 1948, when antibiotics caused a sharp decline in reported cases. The number of reported cases increased during the 1960s and '70s and peaked again, at 1192, in 1981. Cases of this disease continue to be reported. From 1994 to 2001 cases ranged from 366 to 831 per year; the average was 498. There were 695 cases in 2001.

Distribution

Until the 1930s, this disease was reported only in the Rocky Mountains, although it also probably occurred undetected in the eastern U.S. By the late 1930s, more cases were reported in eastern, southeastern, south-central, and southwestern states than in

Rocky Mountain states. The tick carrier in these eastern and southern states is the American dog tick. Since 1963, more than 90% of all cases have been recorded east of the Rocky Mountains. From 1981 to 1992, most cases were reported from Oklahoma, North Carolina, South Carolina, Tennessee, and Arkansas. Rocky Mountain spotted fever is found in all states except Maine, Vermont, Alaska, and Hawaii. More persons are now exposed to infected ticks in the South and East than in Rocky Mountain states. Over the years, clearing and cultivation of wooded land has limited the number and distribution of ticks. Because the ticks and the disease are now found in remote areas, people, mostly men, are not as exposed as in the past. In the South Atlantic and south-central states, the disease is found in men, children, and women who contact infected American dog ticks in their yards, recreational areas, and on their pets. In 1987, four cases of Rocky Mountain spotted fever were reported in the Bronx. Infected persons had not traveled outside New York City within the three weeks before they showed symptoms of the disease.

In the past, in the Rocky Mountains, the disease was found mostly in men who spent time in the woods, hunting, prospecting, exploring, etc. where ticks lived.

Symptoms

The first symptoms of Rocky Mountain spotted fever include fever, severe headache, nausea, and general muscle aches and pains. In a few days, a rash of reddish-purple-black spots appears on the soles of the feet, ankles, palms of the hands, wrists, and forearms in about 80% of cases. This rash may later spread to the trunk, neck, and face. At the end of a week, without treatment, a person may show rapid breathing, become highly agitated, develop insomnia, become delirious, or go into a coma. Recovery in less severe cases may take weeks or months. Appropriate antibiotics given early in the disease are very effective. With early treatment, recovery takes a few days and there are usually no lasting effects. Early treatment can reduce the mortality rate from 25% to about 4%.

Even though this disease has several well-defined clinical symptoms, it is difficult to determine if an illness is Rocky Mountain spotted fever. Specific blood tests can confirm the diagnosis, but, because of the possibility of death, treatment should not be delayed if Rocky Mountain spotted fever is suspected.

Tick carriers and the disease cycle

The Rocky Mountain wood tick, the American dog tick, and the Pacific Coast tick carry the rickettsia that causes Rocky Mountain spotted fever. As a larva, nymph, or adult feeds on an infected animal, it can become infected. An infected larva molts to an infected nymph, and an infected nymph molts to an infected adult. Infected adults feed on people, who become ill with Rocky Mountain spotted fever. Also, an infected female tick can pass the rickettsiae to her eggs.

Since she can lay thousands of eggs, one female tick infected with Rocky Mountain spotted fever may produce thousands of infected larvae.

The rickettsia that causes Rocky Mountain spotted fever can also get into a person's body through the skin—a tick bite is not necessary. People can get Rocky Mountain spotted fever if they crush an attached tick and blood or infected fluids from the tick get into a wound, cut, sore, or in the eye.

People can also get the disease if they handle an infected wild animal or pet, and get urine, blood, or other fluids from the animal on them.

In the Rocky Mountains, Rocky Mountain spotted fever is a disease of late spring and early summer, when adult Rocky Mountain wood ticks are active. In contrast, east of the Rockies, cases of the disease occur throughout spring and summer, when adult American dog ticks are active. Ninety percent of all cases occur between April and September.

Chapter 6.
Other Diseases

A. Human ehrlichiosis

Three related human ehrlichioses are the most recently discovered tick-carried human diseases in the U.S. Three types of this disease have been found: human monocytic ehrlichiosis (HME), human granulocytic ehrlichiosis (HGE), and, most recently, a third ehrlichiosis caused by *Ehrlichia ewingii.*

The first reported case of HME, caused by *Ehrlichia chaffeensis,* occurred in Arkansas in 1986. Since then over 600 cases of HME have been reported from some 30 states. In 2001, 142 cases were reported with highest numbers in Arkansas, Georgia, Missouri, Oklahoma, Tennessee, Texas, and Virginia. Most cases occur in the spring and early summer.

Symptoms of HME include low to high fever, severe headaches, aches and pains in the joints and muscles, chills, loss of appetite, eye pain, nausea, and vomiting. Usually there is no rash. Symptoms can range from very mild (in most cases) to so severe that the person needs hospitalization. Physicians can use specific antibiotics to treat this disease, and early treatment is most effective. Diagnosis requires specific blood tests.

🕷

The lone star tick is the known carrier of HME, but disease organisms have also been found in the American dog tick.

HGE was first diagnosed in patients in Wisconsin and Minnesota in 1993. Since then cases have been found in a number of states, especially where the blacklegged tick and the western blacklegged tick are found. In 2001 there were 261 cases reported; the highest numbers occurred in Minnesota, New York, Massachusetts, and Rhode Island. Recently the disease organism that causes HGE has been identified as *Anaplasma phagocytophilum*. Symptoms of this disease—fever, severe headache, chills, muscle aches, etc.—are similar to symptoms for HME. This disease organism can be identified through specific blood tests. The blacklegged tick, the western blacklegged tick, and the American dog tick carry HGE. Many cases have very mild symptoms, but cases with more severe symptoms respond to early, specific antibiotic treatment.

Most recently, another ehrlichiosis was found in a few cases in Missouri, Oklahoma, and Tennessee. This disease, which has symptoms similar to those of the other human ehrlichioses, is caused by *Ehrlichia ewingii*. Diagnosis and treatment of this disease are similar to those for the other ehrlichioses. The disease organism has been found in lone star ticks and American dog ticks, but little is known about this disease and its tick carriers.

Information on these human ehrlichioses is scarce. Of concern is the multiple co-infection of persons in northern states with the organisms that cause Lyme disease, HGE, and babesiosis. Scientists are learning more about these diseases daily with the promise that practical solutions to the problems caused by these diseases should be available in the future.

B. Southern Tick-Associated Rash Illness

An illness with a rash similar to the rash often associated with Lyme disease has been frequently found in persons in the southeastern and south-central states. This illness has been named Southern Tick-Associated Rash Illness (STARI). Spirochetes like those that cause Lyme disease have not been found in patients with the rash, but a new spirochete, named *Borrelia lonestari*, has been found in 1 to 3% of the lone star ticks tested. It is suspected that this spirochete causes the characteristic rash of Lyme disease, but does not cause Lyme disease itself. However, a mild Lyme disease-like illness may accompany the rash, and antibiotic treatment, as prescribed by a physician, may be appropriate. The incidence and distribution of this illness are at this time unknown.

The lone star tick has a large area of distribution and is an aggressive tick, so Southern Tick-Associated Rash Illness could possibly become widespread in the southeastern United States.

C. Tularemia

Tularemia, also called rabbit fever or deer fly fever, first described in the western U.S. in 1911, is caused by a bacterium, *Francisella tularensis*. Reported cases of tularemia declined from a high of 2291 in 1939 to fewer than 200 per year in the 1970s. The number of reported cases has fallen dramatically. In 1994, the last year official records were kept by CDC, only 85 cases were reported. Unofficially, there were 129 cases reported in 2001, with most cases found in Missouri, Illinois, and Arkansas. Tularemia is found in almost every state.

Symptoms of tularemia include abrupt onset of chills and fever, loss of appetite, weakness, and swollen lymph nodes. Usually there is an ulcer-like wound at the site of the tick bite. If the disease is not diagnosed and treated with specific antibiotics, the symptoms can become more severe. The disease can be diagnosed by identifying the bacterium and by specific blood tests. Tularemia causes a few deaths each year, but early treatment with appropriate antibiotics is effective.

The Rocky Mountain wood tick, the American dog tick, the Pacific Coast tick, and the lone star tick carry tularemia. Ticks feed on infected mice, rabbits, and other animals, molt to the next stage, and these infected ticks give bacteria to hosts as they feed. Infected female ticks can pass bacteria to their larvae through their eggs. Other blood-sucking insects, such as horse flies, deer flies, and mosquitoes, can also carry tularemia.

People can also get tularemia when they handle diseased animals. Rabbit hunters need to be very careful with rabbits they kill. Also, tularemia organisms can enter through the skin if a person crushes an infected tick. Most cases of tularemia are found in the spring and summer, when ticks and other carriers are active, and in the fall, when hunters contact infected rabbits.

Because of its high infectivity, ease of transmission, and potential to cause severe disease, tularemia is considered a possible agent of bioterrorism.

D. Colorado tick fever

This disease, first thought to be a variety of Rocky Mountain spotted fever, was shown to be a separate disease in the 1940s. Colorado tick fever is caused by a virus. Since 1946, the number of reported cases of Colorado tick fever has ranged from 200 to 400 per year. Many cases are not reported because of the mild symptoms. Cases have been reported in California, Colorado, Idaho, Montana, Nevada, New Mexico, Oregon, South Dakota, Utah, Washington, and Wyoming. The disease occurs in altitudes from about 4000 to 10,000 feet.

Symptoms include a sudden high fever, fatigue, chills, severe headache, and muscle aches. The fever may last for one to three days and return suddenly in one to two days. There is no distinct purple-red-black rash, as seen in Rocky Mountain spotted fever, although sometimes there is a faint rash. Other symptoms may include stiff neck, irritation, loss of memory, and loss of coordination. No specific drug is used to treat Colorado tick fever, although treatment for headache and muscle pains may be given. Infected persons usually recover within two weeks without treatment, but in some cases recovery may take several months. This disease can be diagnosed by virus identification and blood tests.

The Rocky Mountain wood tick is the only carrier of Colorado tick fever. Most cases occur in spring and early summer, when adults of this tick are active.

E. Human babesiosis

In the U.S. the first case of human babesiosis, caused by a malaria-like protozoan, *Babesia microti*, was reported on Nantucket Island in 1969. Since then more than 450 cases of babesia infections have been confirmed in the U.S. About 10 to 25 cases are reported each year. Cases have been found in Connecticut, Massachusetts, New Jersey, New York, Rhode Island, Minnesota, Wisconsin, and Georgia. Recently a few cases, caused by another babesia parasite, have been reported in Washington and California. There has been one case reported in Missouri.

Symptoms include fatigue, loss of appetite, fever, chills, sweats, weakness, headache, vomiting, nausea, and muscle aches. In severe cases there is anemia, jaundice, and blood in the urine. Mild symptoms usually go away without treatment, but symptoms may be very severe and babesiosis can cause death in elderly people and in those without a spleen. The disease can be diagnosed by finding disease organisms in the blood or by specific blood tests. Drugs used to treat malaria and certain antibiotics can be used to treat babesiosis. As a complicating factor, persons in the northeast could be infected with Lyme disease, human granulocytic ehrlichiosis, and human babesiosis at the same time.

In the northeast and Midwest, the blacklegged tick carries human babesiosis. Most cases are found from May through July when people are outdoors and blacklegged ticks are active. The tick carrier in the West is not known but the western blacklegged tick is suspected.

F. Tick-borne relapsing fever

Tick-borne relapsing fever (TBRF), found only in the western U.S., is caused by a *Borrelia* spirochete carried by the four kinds of relapsing fever ticks. Only a few cases are reported each year; a total of 450 cases were identified in 11 western states from 1977 to 2000. TBRF is usually found in limited outbreaks in which a few persons in a single location all get the disease at the same time. Also, TBRF has been reported in persons who had been exploring caves.

TBRF takes its name from the high fever that comes and goes in cycles. This high fever lasts from two to nine days and is followed by two to four days without fever, and then the person relapses into another period of high fever. Periods of high fever may show up months after the start of the disease. Antibiotics can be used to treat TBRF. There are no records of death as the result of this disease. TBRF can be diagnosed by finding disease organisms in the blood and by specific blood tests.

Relapsing fever ticks are found in the nests of mice, squirrels, chipmunks, and other small animals. These animals often build their nests in and around cabins or shelters. When the animals are killed or driven out, the remaining ticks become hungry and feed, especially at night, on people who happen to be there. Ticks with disease organisms in their bodies give the disease to the persons they feed on. There are numerous reports of multiple cases of the disease in a group of persons who spent the night together in previously unoccupied cabins without protecting themselves from ticks.

Relapsing fever ticks are also known to feed on persons who enter into caves that house small animals.

G. Q fever

Q fever, short for query fever, also called Nine-Mile fever, is caused by a rickettsia, *Coxiella burnetii*. It is found widely scattered throughout the world, but rarely in the U.S. There were 1936 cases reported from 1948 to 1986 in almost every state. In 2001, 48 cases were reported. Usually the disease appears in distinct outbreaks among persons in the same area or occupation, and is often associated with slaughter houses and farm environments.

Symptoms may occur suddenly and last for one to four weeks, and include severe headaches and a low pulse rate. There is no rash and the disease is usually mild. Antibiotics can be used to treat the disease. Diagnosis is made by the isolation of disease organisms from the blood and specific blood tests.

Q fever organisms have been discovered in the Rocky Mountain wood tick, the Pacific Coast tick, and the lone star tick, but persons rarely get this disease from a tick bite. In laboratory studies, the Rocky Mountain wood tick became infected by feeding on infected hosts and infected females passed the disease organism onto their larvae through the eggs. The organism that causes Q fever is very infective and can enter the body through the skin. Persons can even get Q fever by inhaling disease organisms. Outbreaks of Q fever have occurred among laboratory workers, veterinarians, and farmers in the U.S.

Because it is highly infectious and can be contracted through the air, Q-fever is considered a possible agent of bioterrorism.

H. Tick paralysis

Tick paralysis is not an infectious disease but a tick-caused problem first reported in the Rocky Mountains in 1912. It is caused by a toxin which a tick injects as it feeds. Cases of tick paralysis have been found in most Rocky Mountain and Pacific coast states, especially Montana, Idaho, Oregon, and Washington. Scattered cases are found in southern and southeastern states.

Symptoms usually appear about 5 to 7 days after a person is exposed to ticks. Paralysis usually starts in the hands and feet, and is followed by loss of coordination and activity in the legs and arms. Next is paralysis of the face, with slurred speech and uncontrolled movements of the eyes. Finally, there is irregular breathing. The inability to breathe and paralysis of the heart muscles leads to death. Symptoms usually appear over a period of eight days and are most severe in children. Paralysis is always associated with the feeding of a tick attached on any part of the body, although the head is most common. Once the tick is removed, symptoms rapidly disappear in reverse order of appearance. Usually there are no lasting aftereffects. In cases of unexplained paralysis, a thorough search of the body should be made to look for a feeding tick.

The Rocky Mountain wood tick is the most common cause of tick paralysis in people in the U.S. The American dog tick, the lone star tick, and the black-legged tick also cause tick paralysis. It is not known why only a very few ticks carry the toxin and cause paralysis. Most cases in the West occur between April and June, when adults of the Rocky Mountain wood tick are active. In the South, East, and northeast, most cases are found from March to August when adults of the other ticks are active. Tick-caused paralysis can also be found in dogs, cattle and other livestock.

A summary of locations of important ticks and diseases or problems caused by these ticks is presented in Table 3.

Table 3. Ticks, locations and diseases or problems in the U.S.

Tick	Location	Disease or problem
Lone star	Southeastern third of the U.S.	Nuisance, Tularemia HMEhrlichiosis, Q fever?, Tick paralysis, STARI
Rocky Mountain wood	Western mountains	Rocky Mountain spotted fever, Tularemia, Colorado tick fever, Tick paralysis, Q fever?
Pacific coast	West Coast	Tularemia, Rocky Mountain spotted fever, Colorado tick fever?
American dog	Eastern half of the U.S. and West Coast	Rocky Mountain spotted fever, Tularemia, Tick paralysis, HMEhrlichiosis
Blacklegged	East, South and upper Midwest	Lyme disease, Human babesiosis, HGEhrlichiosis, Tick paralysis
Western black-legged	West Coast	Lyme disease, HGEhrlichiosis, Human babesiosis?
Brown dog	Everywhere	Nuisance
Relapsing fever	West and Florida	Tick-borne Relapsing fever
Pajahuello	California, Nevada	Painful bite

Chapter 7.
How to Protect Yourself

You can avoid tick-carried diseases and tick-caused problems by making sure you do not get ticks on you in the first place. You could stay away from woods, recreational areas, lawns, and other places, even your own yard, where ticks live. However, ticks can even be found in houses, brought in by pets. Unlike other hard ticks, brown dog ticks can survive and reproduce in houses or other places where dogs live. Although this tick does not carry any major human disease in the U.S., it can be a nuisance. If brown dog ticks are hungry and cannot find dogs to feed on, they may attach to people.

You usually find hard ticks outdoors. Their normal hosts are mice, rabbits, birds, deer, and other wild animals. You can see them on you, however, when they are hungry and find you instead of their normal hosts. Some ticks find hosts by waiting on grass or shrubs along paths used by animals. When a host passes, the ticks get on it. Other ticks find hosts by crawling to the host when it is resting or slowly passing by.

It is difficult to avoid ticks when they are seeking a host.

You rarely find relapsing fever ticks outside the nests and burrows of their normal hosts. They leave these places only if they are hungry and their normal hosts are gone. Usually people have to be very near before these ticks find them. Outbreaks of tick-borne relapsing fever usually occur when people have stayed in cabins and shelters that also housed small animals that had relapsing fever ticks feeding on them. Cases of tick-borne relapsing fever have also been found in those who have been in caves. You usually find the pajahuello tick in resting places and bedding grounds of cattle and deer under trees and shrubs. People contact this tick when they walk through or rest in these areas.

You have to make some decisions about what you are going to do about ticks and tick-carried diseases. You should enjoy nature but that enjoyment is not without risks. If you think the risk of getting a tick-carried disease is great, you may decide to avoid an area completely and not expose yourself to the danger. If you decide to expose yourself to ticks and diseases, you can use the measures described in this chapter to reduce your contact with ticks. If you use them properly, these measures will greatly reduce your risk of getting tick bites and a tick-carried disease.

A. Proper Clothing

You can prevent tick attachment or reduce the number of ticks that attach to you by removing them before they attach. You should wear light-colored clothing so ticks are visible on your clothes. Wear a long-sleeved shirt that fits tightly at the wrists and neck and tuck the shirt into your pants, and wear long pants with the legs tucked into your boots or your socks. You could even use masking tape to tape the pant legs tightly to your socks, shoes, or boots. Ticks tend to crawl upward, and these measures are to keep ticks on the outside of your clothes, so you can see and remove them before they reach your skin and attach. Wearing long-sleeved shirts and long pants can be very hot in the summer, and it may be especially impossible to keep them on children. Unfortunately, wearing them is warranted if there is a threat of a tick-carried disease in your region, and you are serious about keeping ticks away from you and your family.

You should check your clothing to make sure it is tick-free before you enter your house. Once inside, it is a good idea to place your clothes on a sheet and examine them carefully or place them in a bag until you wash and dry them as soon as possible. Ticks in your house may attach to you later, when you are not expecting it.

You should inspect your pets when they come in to make sure they are tick-free. If you find ticks, you can remove them carefully (Chapter 8), or you can treat your pet with an approved insecticide (Chapter 9).

Despite all your efforts, ticks may still get to your skin. Some people can feel ticks crawling on them; most cannot. A good practice is to shower or bathe and to check your body for ticks, especially in areas that have hair or where clothing was tight, as soon as possible after coming indoors. You should inspect yourself visually and by hand. If possible, have another person examine you to make sure you have not missed any ticks. You will usually see bigger ticks—nymphs and adults. Pick them off if they have not attached, or else carefully remove them if they have already attached (Chapter 8). It is difficult to see and remove larvae (seed ticks). Usually you notice them only after they have attached and their feeding has caused the skin at the attachment site to itch. You can scrape them off or you can treat the places where they are attached with medications that are available to treat the body for lice.

Though it is difficult, you should try to protect children with proper clothes, if possible. Whether you can or cannot, it is important that you thoroughly bathe and inspect children, and remove any crawling or attached ticks promptly.

B. Repellents Applied to Skin and Clothing

You can decrease the number of ticks that reach your skin and attach by treating your body or clothing with a repellent. The most common, EPA-registered, and effective repellent for ticks, chiggers, mosquitoes, and other pests is deet (*N,N*-diethyl-*meta*-toluamide). Deet has been marketed in the U.S. since 1956 and millions of people use it each year. You can buy this repellent under many trade names; it is available in sticks, lotions, creams, solutions, and pump or aerosol spray cans. Thoroughly read the label of any repellent product to make sure it contains deet and apply as directed for maximum effectiveness and safety.

You can apply certain products that contain deet directly to your skin to repel ticks, mosquitoes, and other biting insects. Ticks that crawl on the treated skin are irritated by the repellent and drop off. However, deet is most effective against ticks when applied to clothing from a spray can. Hang up your shirt and pants or lay them on the ground, hold the can about a foot or less from the clothes and spray each side of each piece for about 15 seconds. You must treat both the front and back thoroughly. If you are already dressed, you can spray your front pretty well, but you should have someone else spray your back. You must avoid getting the product in your eyes. Treat footwear, socks, and pant cuffs for protection at these critical places. Follow label instructions exactly.

In tests, volunteers applied a repellent that contained 20% deet to their shirts and pants and walked through or sat in tick-infested areas for between 30 minutes and an hour. They determined protection by recording the numbers of ticks that reached their skin. The treatment provided about 85% protection against the lone star tick and the blacklegged tick and 94% protection against the American dog tick. In other tests, a repellent that contained 30% deet afforded 93% protection against the blacklegged tick. In all these tests, the volunteers taped their pants to or tucked them inside their socks or boots. Ticks had to stay on the outside of the clothing, where they were exposed to the repellent.

Do not apply repellents that contain deet to rayon, spandex or synthetic fibers other than nylon. They may damage furniture finishes, plastics, painted surfaces, and plastic watch crystals.

Generally, repellents containing deet last on the skin for a limited number of hours. Recently, a new controlled release formulation of deet has been tested and found to repel ticks and to prevent attachment for up to 72 hours.

Deet is a widely used repellent, but some people have reported adverse toxic reactions, such as seizures, allergic responses, and skin irritation. To reduce the possibility of these reactions you should do the following:

- apply deet sparingly to your skin,
- avoid applying high-concentration products (those with greater than 30% deet) to the skin, particularly of children,
- not inhale or ingest deet products or get them into your eyes,
- apply deet to clothes to reduce exposure to deet,
- avoid treating parts of children's hands that may contact their eyes or mouth,
- not treat wounds or irritated skin, and
- wash treated skin after coming indoors.

If a reaction occurs, you should wash your skin and take the repellent product with you when you see a physician.

C. Toxicants Applied to Clothing

The EPA has registered only one toxicant to be applied to clothing to control ticks. Permethrin, an insecticide, is sold under several trade names, such as Permanone®, Duranon®, and others, as aerosol sprays or as non-aerosol pump sprays. These products are available throughout the U.S. Permethrin is called a tick repellent because it kills ticks so rapidly that the ticks appear to be repelled.

Label instructions call for thorough treatment of clothing before dressing. You must allow the clothing to dry for two to four hours before putting it on. You should not treat your bare skin or the clothing on your body with this insecticide.

Volunteers applied this insecticide to their clothing and tested the product against ticks as they did in the tests with deet. The treatment provided 100% protection against the lone star tick, the American dog tick, the Pacific Coast tick, the blacklegged tick, and the western blacklegged tick. In laboratory tests, Coulston's Permethrin® Tick Repellent applied to a cloth killed the pajahuello tick.

Ticks that crawl on treated clothing for only a few seconds drop off and most of them die. Usually a single treatment will protect against ticks for up to six weeks even after weekly laundering. Carefully read and follow the label directions exactly. You must not apply permethrin directly to your skin, face, or eyes. If you accidentally should get some on you, you must wash it off quickly with soap and water. If you get it into your eyes, flush them with plenty of water.

Chapter 8.
How to Remove Ticks

Despite all your efforts, you have found a tick attached to your skin or someone else's skin. What do you do? You should remove a tick as soon as possible after you discover it. Ticks in the process of attaching are easier to remove than firmly attached ticks. More importantly, usually an infected tick must be attached for a day or longer for it to inject disease organisms into its host. The sooner you find and remove an attached tick, the less chance you have of getting a disease the tick may be carrying.

You must remove attached ticks properly for two reasons. First, you must be certain to remove all the mouthparts from your skin. A tick attaches by inserting its hypostome, shaped like a harpoon with many recurved barbs (Figure 1), into the skin. If you remove the tick improperly, the mouthparts may break off, remain in the skin, and can become the site of irritation and secondary infection. Second, the organisms that cause Rocky Mountain spotted fever, tularemia, and Q fever can enter your body through the skin, and if you crush or break an attached tick that contains these organisms, the disease organism may get into your body. You must remove attached ticks carefully so that you do not break off their mouthparts or puncture or crush them.

The lone star tick has the longest mouthparts of all the ticks listed in this book and is the most difficult to remove. The degree of difficulty in removing an attached tick depends upon the length of the mouthparts, the amount of cement secreted, the stage of the tick (mouthparts of adults are longer than those of nymphs, which are longer than those of larvae), and the length of time the tick has been feeding. Some people react to an attached tick by swelling at the site; this swelling may make it more difficult to remove the tick.

We all have heard of special methods to remove attached ticks. Some claim these folk methods will cause ticks to back out of or detach from the skin. In one study researchers allowed adult American dog ticks to attach to sheep. After three or four days, they covered some ticks with petroleum jelly, some with clear nail polish, and others with rubbing alcohol. They also treated a few by lighting a wooden kitchen match, blowing it out, and touching the tick with the hot, smoking end of the match. None of these folk methods made the ticks detach. In contrast, researchers removed other attached ticks by grasping them with protected fingers or with blunt curved forceps or tweezers as closely as possible to where the mouthparts entered the skin and steadily pulling the ticks from the skin. They found no crushed ticks or broken mouthparts. They obtained the same results with ticks that had been attached for only 12 to 15 hours.

Researchers also allowed adult lone star ticks, which have much longer mouthparts than American dog ticks, to attach to sheep. They grasped the ticks with blunt curved forceps or tweezers as close to the skin as possible. They pulled some ticks steadily away from the skin, others with a jerk, and others with a twisting motion. Finally they pulled some parallel to the skin. The most effective method, in which no ticks were crushed and no mouthparts broken, was the steady direct pull away from the skin.

In the past several years, a number of devices which claim to aid in removing attached ticks have been marketed. You will find they are designed in two different ways to remove attached ticks. The forceps type, such as the Tick Solution®, the De-Ticker®, the Silver Gripper®, and Tick-X Tick Extractor®, which may or may not be spring loaded, are designed to help you grasp the mouthparts of the tick. The Tick Nipper®, also called the Tick Plier®, is a plastic pliers-shaped device you use to grasp the tick. The other type, such as Ticked Off®, a deep, bowl-shaped plastic spoon, the Pro-tick Remedy®, an almost flat stainless steel spoon, and the O'Tom® Tick Remover, a hooked-shaped device, have a V-shaped notch you slip around the tick's mouthparts between the tick and the skin. As you push the tick farther into the notch and apply increasing upward pressure, you eventually lift the tick from the skin. Finally, a unique device, the Trix® Tick Remover Pen, has a plastic loop on the end you can extend around an attached tick. You tightly close the loop around the tick's mouthparts and remove the tick with a rotating action. Recent studies have shown that the Tick Nipper®, Ticked Off® and the Pro-Tick Remedy® removed adult American dog ticks and lone star ticks. None of these devices, including medium tipped forceps, removed nymphal ticks without damage to their mouthparts.

The best way to remove an attached tick is as follows:

1. Use blunt curved forceps, tweezers or an appropriate tick tweezers-type removal device. If you must use your fingers, cover them with rubber gloves, waxed paper, plastic, or paper toweling.
2. Place the tips of the tweezers or your fingers or the edges of the devices around the tick's mouthparts where they enter the skin.
3. Remove the tick with a steady pull away from the skin—do not jerk or twist the tick.
4. If you use devices with the V-notch, slide the mouthparts of the tick into the notch, add slight pressure downward on the skin, slide the device forward until the mouthparts are tightly surrounded on three sides by the device, and lift the tick from the skin.
5. Take great care not to crush or puncture the body of the tick or get any fluids from the tick on you.
6. Examine the attachment site carefully to make sure you have removed all of the mouthparts.
7. If you wish to keep the tick alive, place it in a sealable container, such as a bag or vial, with moist paper and store it in the refrigerator. You may give it to a person who knows about ticks for examination if you suspect the possibility of a tick-carried disease.
8. After you have removed the tick, disinfect your skin with alcohol or povidone iodine and wash your hands with soap and water.

Chapter 9.
How to Control Ticks

You live in an area that has ticks and tick-carried diseases. It also has an abundance of mice, deer, and other wildlife as hosts for ticks. You should know that you can use a variety of materials and methods to decrease the numbers of ticks in your home and community, and thus decrease the opportunity for you to become infected with a tick-carried disease. You can do something on your own property, and you can also be active in initiating and supporting community-wide, larger-scale programs to decrease the number of ticks in your area. Keeping your property free of ticks is a difficult job. You may need constantly to reapply control measures, as ticks can come back onto your property from neighboring areas if they are not being controlled there. Community-wide projects, however, have the potential to decrease the numbers of ticks in much larger areas for a longer period of time. These projects are usually maintained by large organizations with trained staff and a mandate to decrease numbers of ticks and tick-carried diseases as defined by agreements and laws.

This chapter will describe a number of tick control materials and methods that can be used both by individuals and organizations.

A. Area Control with Insecticides

Other than personal protection, the most common way to fight ticks is to treat with insecticides the places ticks live.

The Environmental Protection Agency (EPA) has registered several insecticides you can apply to houses, kennels, yards, and other places to control the brown dog tick. Some of these insecticides are registered to control the brown dog tick only, while most are also registered to control the brown dog tick and other ticks found outside the house. A few other insecticides can be used only by pest control operators, public-health officials, or other certified, registered personnel.

Even though ticks are not insects, they are usually killed by the same insecticides that kill insects, you can apply insecticides safely and effectively to kill them.

You should be able to obtain a list of registered insecticides you can use to control ticks on your property from your local county agricultural extension agents or advisors, public health personnel, or other officials. They should also have information on how you can use these insecticides safely and effectively. Because of the ongoing changes that take place in the list of registered insecticides, this book presents only general information on using insecticides effectively and safely.

You can buy insecticides in pet shops, feed stores, garden shops, nurseries, grocery stores, discount stores, and many other places. In most of these stores you will find a number of products on the shelves, but often no one who knows how to select and use them. It is up to you to choose the correct one.

The label on an insecticide can, bottle, or package contains all the information you need to select and use it correctly. You must read the label thoroughly so you will know if the product is registered to control the brown dog tick only, or to control it and other ticks. The label will tell how and where to apply the insecticide. If you don't follow the instructions exactly, the treatment may be ineffective, damage the environment, or be toxic to you, pets, and wildlife. The label also contains information on hazards to persons and animals, practical treatments for accidental exposure, precautions and environmental hazards, and instructions for proper storage and disposal of the container.

You will find some insecticides sold as ready-to-use products you can apply directly from the container. Others are liquid concentrates or wettable powders you must dilute with water before use. The label gives exact instructions on how to dilute the concentrate or powder. Some are available as granules you can sprinkle onto areas that have ticks.

To control the brown dog tick, you must treat the dog and the area in which it lives. Treating the dog will kill ticks attached to the dog and treating where the dog lives will kill ticks that are laying eggs, molting, or looking for a host. Veterinarians can prescribe several special insecticides to be used as oral or dermal treatments to be applied to pets to control ticks and fleas as well. You can treat a dog by washing or dipping it, applying the insecticide down the backline or to a spot on the back, or you can use an insecticidal collar. You must thoroughly spray baseboards, window and door frames, and cracks on the floors where the dog lives. You should remove all bedding and replace it with fresh bedding after treating the dog and where the dog lives and runs. If your dogs run outdoors, treat the ground and other places where they live and play. You may have to treat several times before you get rid of brown dog ticks.

You can control the other hard ticks listed in Chapter 3 by applying insecticides to the environment. Follow label instructions exactly. You can apply insecticides as sprays directly onto weeds, shrubs, underbrush, and nearby grassy areas. Treat with enough volume to wet plants and the ground thoroughly. Spray along footpaths and roadsides where ticks congregate. You can also apply insecticides as granules which penetrate growing vegetation and end up on the ground where ticks live. Do not allow children or pets to go into treated areas until the spray has dried. Because some insecticides are toxic to fish, you must not treat lakes, streams, or ponds. Do not pollute water by cleaning equipment or disposing of waste insecticide in any body of water.

You may have to keep your dog out of the house to prevent reinfestation.

You can treat for ticks any time of the year, but for it to be most effective, you should treat when ticks are most likely to be active in your area. A treatment applied in the late spring will kill ticks that have overwintered. A treatment applied in the late summer will kill larvae that have hatched from eggs, nymphs that have molted from larvae, and adults that have molted from nymphs that fed during the summer. You may have to treat at intervals throughout the summer if tick numbers are high and there is a threat of disease in your area. A treatment applied in the fall will decrease the number of ticks that overwinter and look for hosts the next spring.

If you suspect you are moving into a shelter or a building that may harbor relapsing fever ticks, you may wish to treat the area with one of the insecticides approved for the control of ticks in houses.

A FINAL, IMPORTANT NOTE: If you choose to use insecticides to control ticks in your house or in the environment, you must follow the label instructions exactly. The label is there to provide you with information so you can use these products safely and effectively. You may prefer to hire a trained, licensed person to apply the insecticide for you.

B. Vegetation Management

You can manage vegetation to control ticks, especially the lone star tick and the blacklegged tick. The purpose of vegetation management is two-fold. The first is to decrease areas covered with shrubs and undergrowth, which are the favorite habitat of wildlife. The other is to remove the leaf litter and duff on the soil, which eliminates the protective layer on the ground where ticks live. Sunlight reaching the ground dries the soil, making it unsuitable for eggs and ticks in the host-seeking stages. Reducing the amount of underbrush and removing the trash and leaf litter from your yard or property will lessen attractiveness as nesting sites for the mice that are hosts of larval blacklegged ticks. You can manage vegetation mechanically by trimming or removing trees to thin out the overstory, removing the understory vegetation (shrubs, brush, tall weeds, etc.), and closely mowing the grass.

You can reduce or remove leaf litter and duff on the soil by controlled burning where permitted. Fire consumes the leaf litter and duff and also kills ticks in that layer and on the soil surface. You can also manage vegetation by applying EPA-registered herbicides to plants according to label instructions.

These different methods of vegetation management require different amounts of money, knowledge, and experience. The easiest to use in a small area is mechanical clearing: trim or cut down certain trees by hand, eliminate understory vegetation with a weed cutter, and mow grasses closely. An effective controlled burn takes a great deal of knowledge, skill, and preparation. You must have enough dead grass, leaves, and other burnable material on the soil to support an effective fire. A fire that burns too quickly and without enough heat will not kill ticks. Unfortunately, fires get out of control easily and can be very dangerous. Herbicides are effective, but you must use them with caution. You must have knowledge, experience, and proper equipment to apply herbicides correctly and safely. Unless you are experienced in the application of any of these measures to control vegetation, it would be best to have the work done by a licensed, registered professional applicator.

C. Insecticide-Treated Nest Material

You can use a product of EcoHealth, Inc. called Damminix® tick tubes to control the blacklegged tick on mice. It consists of a cardboard tube that contains cotton treated with permethrin—the same insecticide found in Permanone®, Duranon®, and certain other tick control products applied to clothing (Chapter 7). Damminix® works by killing larvae and nymphs on mice. Mice live on the ground and make nests out of leaves, grass, loose debris, etc. Mice take the treated cotton from the tubes to make their nests and the insecticide on the cotton kills ticks on the mice while in their nests.

Damminix® is only effective when you place the tubes where mice live. The label calls for placing tubes at 10-yard intervals. This spacing is critical, as it puts tubes within the home range of most mice. Place tubes on the ground at the edges of lawns, in gardens, and other areas where you find mice. The cotton should stay dry, as mice prefer to nest in dry, fluffy material. You should treat with Damminix® twice each year. The first treatment, in April or May, kills the overwintered larvae and nymphs; the second, in July or August, kills the larvae that have hatched in the summer. The recommended treatment is 48 tubes per acre where you find mice. This product has been used extensively, but, unfortunately, there have been conflicting results reported as to its effectiveness in reducing the numbers of host-seeking nymphs of the blacklegged tick the next spring.

Damminix® is registered with the EPA and is only available in California, Connecticut, Maryland, Massachusetts, New Hampshire, New Jersey, New York, Pennsylvania, Rhode Island, and Virginia.

D. Bait and Insecticide Treatment of Mice

A somewhat similar treatment has recently been developed to attract mice with a bait into a small plastic chamber that contains the insecticide fipronil. In the chamber the mice are lightly treated with the insecticide to kill the ticks on them. This device and treatment method is called the Maxforce Tick Management System, a product of Bayer Environmental Science.

Personnel of the CDC, in cooperation with those of the company, tested this device in Connecticut and found an 80% reduction in the number of nymphal blacklegged ticks after the first year and 96% reduction after two years. Instructions call for placing the chambers 30 feet apart at the edge of maintained landscaping, wood lots, and/or brush in the spring and then replacing them after 90 days for a second treatment. The EPA has approved this product under special provisions of the Federal Insecticide, Fungicide and Rodenticide Act for use only by registered and trained pest management specialists.

E. Deer Treatment

Another new device which is now available is the four-poster deer treatment bait station, developed to control ticks on deer. This device consists of a central bin which contains shelled corn. This corn is metered to the ends of the device where it becomes available to deer in two troughs. As the deer bends to pick up the corn, it has to place its head, neck, and shoulders against applicator rollers (on two posts at each end of the device, thus the name "four-poster") that are treated with insecticide. The insecticide kills the ticks on the body of the deer where it has rubbed against the rollers. The deer treats other parts of its body through grooming.

USDA scientists in Texas have extensively tested this device and found it provided over 90% control of lone star ticks after three years of use. Other researchers tested it in Maryland and found it reduced the numbers of free-living blacklegged ticks by over 95% after three years of treatment. Researchers have conducted a very large field test in Connecticut, Maryland, New Jersey, New York, and Rhode Island to control the blacklegged tick. The results of this test are presently being evaluated.

The American Lyme Disease Foundation, Inc. has now commercially developed this device. Since four-poster devices effectively treat deer in large areas, devices will be sold only in groups of nine in order to treat deer in 350- to 450-acre areas. Depending upon use, operators of the devices will need to replace both the corn in the bin and the insecticide on the applicators at weekly or bi-weekly intervals. Only pest control operators or licensed pesticide applicators are approved for application of a special formulation of the insecticide, permethrin, approved for use in the devices.

F. Deer Management

Since ticks that carry diseases feed on wild animals, especially adult ticks on deer, to get rid of or to decrease the number of ticks, the simplest method of control is to eliminate or decrease the number of deer. In studies with the lone star tick, researchers kept deer out of a small area with a deer-proof fence and saw a 98% decrease in the number of larvae inside the area. There was only a small decrease however, in the number of adults and nymphs. This lack of effectiveness against these stages of ticks was because they could have fed on medium-sized wild animals, such as raccoons, foxes, or skunks, not excluded by the fence. They found an increase in the number of American dog ticks in the area. In other tests, they built a deer-proof fence around a large campsite, and also used vegetative management and insecticides in limited areas of the site. They recorded a reduction in the number of larval and nymphal lone star ticks inside the deer-free, treated area, but no decrease in the number of American dog ticks.

In studies with the blacklegged tick, researchers removed about 70% of the deer from an island and saw no reduction in the number of blacklegged tick larvae on mice the next summer. They removed all the deer and saw a rapid decrease in the number of larvae. Because the life cycle of the blacklegged tick takes two years, it takes a while to see the effects of the removal of deer on the population of this tick.

Recent studies with standard deer-proof fencing and special electric fencing to exclude deer showed decreased numbers of host-seeking, disease-carrying blacklegged ticks. These fences are expensive to construct and maintain, but the cost may be justified for a specific area if ticks and the diseases they carry are reduced or eliminated. Deer are accepted and wanted wildlife, however, and it seems unlikely people will give up their deer.

G. Integrated Pest Management

A final word should be said about integrating the materials and methods listed in this chapter. Each technique has its benefits and problems. Insecticide application generally gives fast control of ticks but may be expensive and must be done correctly to be effective and safe. Some people choose not to use insecticides around their homes. Vegetation management is less effective, slower acting, and requires special equipment, but may be longer lasting. You may need to repeat major vegetation management activities every three or four years. Mouse treatment with nesting material or bait can be very effective if used correctly. Deer treatment for two or three years may provide excellent control of ticks, but must be done by trained, certified persons, can be expensive, and requires a large area to be effective. Deer management is the slowest-acting, and it may be necessary to eliminate all deer in a large area for a long period of time (probably an impossible task) to affect the number of ticks.

You may need to repeat insecticide treatments yearly or more often.

Individual property owners can use two or more of these tick control techniques to reduce the tick population on their property. An example would be the integration of some type of vegetative management, such as brush removal or close mowing of the lawn, with the use of a mouse treatment technique to reduce numbers of blacklegged ticks around an individual house. Area control with insecticides could be combined with vegetative management. A group of property owners could each use the same small scale techniques to reduce the number of ticks in their neighborhood. Other techniques, such as deer treatment or management, are only effective if used in large scale programs to reduce numbers of ticks in an area as large as a town, township, park, recreation area, etc. Combining and integrating several techniques on both small and large scale has the potential to reduce the number of ticks and thus the diseases and other problems caused by ticks.

Appendix
Useful Websites

This little book presents practical, factual information, without much detail, on ticks, the diseases they carry, and materials and methods you can use to protect yourself from ticks and these diseases. Interested readers may choose to obtain more information on one or more of the subjects listed in this book. Certainly a library is a good source of books that contain more detailed information. Probably the greatest modern source of information is the Internet. For example, if you go to a search engine, such as Google or Compuserve, and call for a search for information on any specific subject, such as Lyme disease, lone star tick, or tick paralysis, you will be presented with thousands of web sites you can go to for further information. In addition, a number of state, national, public, and private organizations, including health organizations and universities, have websites that contain very general to very specific information on ticks and tick-carried diseases. Unfortunately, websites present a wide variety of information which can vary greatly in accuracy and quality. It is critical that you seek confirmation of information you obtain from the Internet by finding it presented in several sources.

The following is a partial list (there are many sites) of websites that the interested reader may use as a starting point in order to find additional information on ticks and tick-carried diseases.

American Academy of Family Physicians:
www.familydoctor.org

American Lyme Disease Foundation, Inc:
www.aldf.com

American Medical Association:
www.ama-assn.org

American Veterinary Medical Association:
www.avma.org

Armed Forces Pest Management Board:
www.afpmb.org

Centers for Disease Control:
www.cdc.gov/ncidod/dvrd

Dept. of Public Health, Massachusetts:
www.state.ma.us/dph (almost all other states have
  similar sites)

Emergency Medicine:
www.eMedicine.com

Harvard Medical School:
www.intelihealth.com

Lyme Disease Association, Inc:
www.lymediseaseassociation.org

Lyme Disease Info Network:
www.lymeinfo.net

Lyme Disease Network of the Lyme Disease Assn, Inc.:
www.lymenet.org

Mayo Clinic:
www.MayoClinic.com

The Merck Manual:
www.merck.com/pubs/mmanual

National Institute of Allergy and Infectious Diseases:
www.niaid.nih.gov

National Library of Medicine:
www.medlineplus.gov

Stop Ticks on People:
www.stopticks.org

List of Illustrations

Index

🕷